Eye On The Environment

POLLUTED AIR

J.M. Patten, Ed.D.

The Rourke Book Co., Inc.
Vero Beach, Florida 32964

Edited by Pamela J.P. Schroeder and Sandra A. Robinson

PHOTO CREDITS
© John Patten: cover, pages 6, 7, 10, 12, 13, 16, 22; courtesy Alaska Commission on the Environment: pages 15, 19; © Robert Visser, Greenpeace: pages 4, 18; © Ron Romanosky, Greenpeace: page 9; © Mike Naylor: page 21

Library of Congress Cataloging-in-Publication Data

Patten, J.M., 1944-
    Polluted air / J.M. Patten.
    p. cm. — (Eye on the environment)
    Includes index.
    ISBN 1-55916-098-5
    1. Air—Pollution—Juvenile literature.
[1. Air—Pollution. 2. Pollution.] I. Title. II. Series.
TD883.13.P38   1995
363.73'92—dc20   94-38616
                                                      CIP
                                                      AC

Printed in the USA

TABLE OF CONTENTS

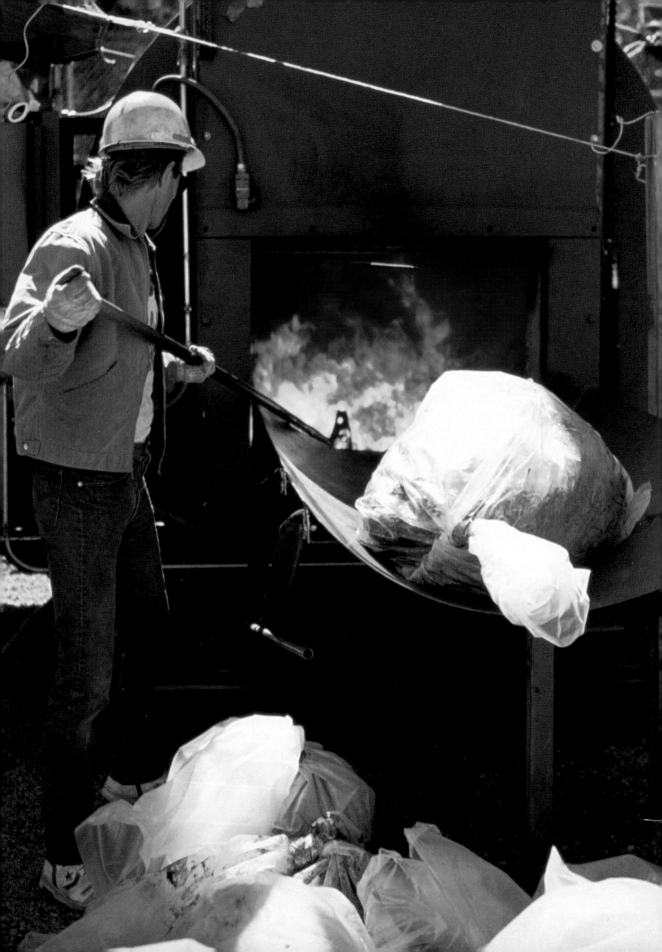

EYE ON AIR POLLUTION

This book is about air pollution. You will find out how clean air becomes **polluted,** or dirty, and harms the Earth's **environment.**

The Earth's environment is all living and nonliving things in the world. The soil we farm, air we breathe, and water we drink are important parts of the environment. People must work to protect them.

Earth is our home—the only known place where people, plants and animals can live. Air pollution damages our home and hurts us all.

A worker burns trash and makes smoke and ash that pollute the air we breathe.

CLEAN AIR

The air we breathe is part of the Earth's **atmosphere.**

People, plants and animals all need air to live. They need clean, clear air to stay healthy and to enjoy life.

The filter on the right removed this much dust from household air in a month—the blue filter is new.

Pump bottles and spray cans—everyday air polluters—are common in every house and garage.

Polluted air is dirty, hazy and smelly. Dust and poisons in dirty air harm people and animals. Polluted air can kill forests and even the crops farmers grow.

AIR POLLUTION AND HEALTH

Air pollution causes many health problems for young and old people. Polluted air causes stinging, running eyes and sneezing.

Breathing dirty air for a long time sometimes can cause serious throat and lung diseases. Diseases like asthma, bronchitis, colds and pneumonia are made worse by waste gases and smoke in the air we breathe. People's lungs last longer and work better when the air they use is clean and clear.

In many cities, people watch for air pollution alerts like they watch for weather reports. When there are high levels of air pollution, TV and radio announcers warn people to stay indoors.

People in this city are breathing the air you see.

8

AIR POLLUTION AND THE ATMOSPHERE

Air pollution is destroying the **ozone layer** in the sky. The ozone layer protects us from harmful sun rays. Where the ozone layer is thin, people must wear hats outside, or harmful sun rays will burn their skin.

Scientists found a hole in the ozone layer over Antarctica in 1985 and have learned the ozone layer is getting thinner and thinner over the north pole.

Luckily, the ozone layer can repair itself if our air is kept clean. People are working harder to keep air free from dangerous pollution to protect the ozone layer.

This swimmer wears a shirt to save his skin from the sun's harmful rays.

FOSSIL FUELS

Coal and oil are called **fossil fuels.** They were formed millions of years ago in the Earth.

Today, people mine—dig up—coal from the ground. Most oil is pumped to the Earth's surface from underground pools.

Small gasoline engines can make more air pollution in an hour than some cars make running all day.

Car engines should be kept in good running shape so they cause less air pollution.

Factories, power stations and cars burn fossil fuels to make energy or power. When fossil fuels burn, they also make waste smoke, dust, dirt and gases that pollute the air.

THE BIGGEST AIR POLLUTERS

Many factories burn coal or oil to run their machines. Factories need fossil fuels to make the things people use at home or work.

Many electric stations use fossil fuels to generate, or make, electricity. We use electricity to heat, cool and light our homes and stores.

Cars, trucks, trains, buses and ships use gasoline for fuel. Gasoline is made from oil— a fossil fuel.

Factories, electric stations, cars and trucks help us in our everyday lives. However, they also hurt us by creating air pollution.

A worker watches a spinning drill on an oil drilling platform.

AIR POLLUTERS BIG AND SMALL

Volcanic eruptions and other huge explosions can pour tons of dirt and dust into the air. This air pollution can circle the Earth high in the atmosphere for months—and even block out some light from the sun.

Cigarette smoke is also air pollution. The government makes sure that every cigarette package has a warning label on it.

Smoke from candles, cooking and cigarettes causes indoor air pollution.

AIR POLLUTION ON THE MOVE

Most air pollution is made in large cities. Smoke and dust may stay over a city for a long time, making **smog.** Smog—hazy air pollution—makes breathing hard. Sometimes people close to big cities are warned not to go outside when smog is very heavy.

Smoke, dust and waste gases pour out of the power station and drift in the wind.

Sunsets look pretty because the sun's light is reflecting off dirt and dust in the air.

The wind blows air pollution many, many miles from where it was made. It can travel to country towns and farms, and damage far-away forests.

STOPPING AIR POLLUTION

Factories and electric stations—big air polluters—can put "scrubbers" on their smokestacks. Scrubbers trap pollution before it can get out into the air we breathe. Electric stations can also wash coal before it's burned to remove pollutants.

Waste gases and smoke from cars and trucks can be kept out of our air by using special anti-pollution parts.

In many areas, outdoor burning of trash and yard wastes is against the law because it pollutes the air.

GLOSSARY

atmosphere (AT muh sfeer) — the air that surrounds the Earth's surface

environment (en VI ren ment) — the world around us including plants, animals, soil, water and air

fossil fuels (FAH suhl FYOOLZ) — fuels that come from the ground, made by nature long ago

polluted (puh LOOT ed) — made dirty and harmful to people, plants and animals

ozone layer (O zone LAY er) — protective layer high in the atmosphere that helps keep out some of the sun's harmful rays

smog (SMAWG) — a mixture of waste gases, vapor and smoke that makes it hard to breathe

Scientists think the dead trees in this forest were killed by a type of air pollution called acid rain.

INDEX